HARRIET TUBMAN
who led slaves to freedom

BY
MRS. GEORGE SCHWAB
first published in 1869

reprinted by
New York History Review
2022

HARRIET TUBMAN who led slaves to freedom
by Mrs. George Schwab, 1869, reprinted by
New York History Review in 2022

ISBN: 978-1-950822-24-9

Printed in the United States of American

Cover photo of Harriet Tubman, photographer unknown.

Table of Contents

Chapter 1. A Slave in Maryland.

Slavery wherever it exists is an evil. In 1619 slavery was introduced into North America when twenty Africans were landed in the state of Virginia.

There are now in the United States of America 13,000,000 descendants of these slaves who have been free men and women since the Emancipation Proclamation of President Lincoln in 1863. This is the story of one of these former slaves.

Harriet Tubman was born about 1820 in a village in the state of Maryland. She was one of eleven children. Her grandparents came from Africa between 1725 and 1750. Some say that they came from Ashanti, others that they were Fellatas. They were slaves working for tobacco planters.

Harriet was a small, thin, very black child. She never went to school.

When she was five years old, she began to work. When she was six, she was taken ten miles away from her home to learn weaving. One day she ran away from her mistress who had whipped her for taking a lump of sugar. She hid from Friday until the next Tuesday. By that time, she was so hungry
that she went back and was flogged by the master of the house.

Some slave owners were good to their slaves but Harriet did not meet them. When she was ill, she was sent home to her mother's hut. She always rebelled against her lot. Her father often said to her, "Child, don't fret so about it all. Heed God and be as good as you best know how to be."

Harriet's parents went to church regularly. They could not read, but they learned parts of the Bible which they taught to their children.

When Harriet heard of a slave's escape from his master she thought of the verse in Isaiah 16:3, "hide the outcasts; betray not the fugitive." The helping of slaves to freedom became her aim in life. When she was still a girl she carried out this aim in spite of many difficulties.

When Harriet was thirteen or fourteen years old she became a worker on a farm. One evening, one of the slaves, instead of working, went to the village store. The overseer followed him and so did Harriet.

When the slave was found, the overseer called on Harriet and others to help tie him. She refused, and as the slave ran away, she stood in the door to stop people from running after him. The overseer threw a two-pound weight at the slave, but it struck Harriet on the head. For the rest of the autumn, she lay ill in her parent's hut. Her master brought buyers to the plantation, hoping to sell her. When they saw her thin face, her wounded head and her weakness, they refused. As Harriet said later, " They wouldn't give a sixpence for me." In the midst of conversation or some household work she would stop and fall asleep. This might happen three or four times a day.

When she woke up she continued her conversation or work where she had left off.

Of this time Harriet said, " from Christmas until March, I worked as I could, and I prayed through the long nights—I prayed for old master, ' Oh Lord, convert master ! Oh Lord, change that man's heart!'"

She prayed always, about her work. When she went to the horse-trough to wash her face she took up the water in her hands and said, " Oh Lord, wash me, make me clean! " Lifting the cloth to dry her face, she asked that all her sins be wiped away.

Taking the broom to sweep, she prayed, " Oh Lord, whatsoever sin there be in my heart, sweep it out. Lord, clear and clean."

Harriet worked for five or six years on the same plantation with her father and became strong. Before she was nineteen years old she was a match for the strongest of the men. She could lift great weights and draw a heavy load like an ox.

Chapter 2. Escape.

There was beginning to be much unrest among the slaves. Stories had come to them of a movement for freedom in the states north of Maryland. There was a line, called the Mason and Dixon line, which had been surveyed by two Englishmen, Charles Mason and Jeremiah Dixon, to mark the boundary between Maryland and Pennsylvania. This line separated the northern or free states from the slaveholding or the southern states. There were white and black men and women in the free states working together against slavery. Both risked their lives to bring slaves across the Mason and Dixon line to freedom. In the time of Harriet's grandparents there was a network of special paths with secret aid to help slaves to go to Canada. This was called the Underground Railroad.

Harriet asked herself "Shall I go to the North or stay in the South?"

About 1844 she married John Tubman, a free Negro, and decided to stay in the South. She still had to work for her master, but at night she could share the hut of her husband. Harriet loved her husband and lived with him about five years before she escaped North. She underwent the dangers of a journey back South two years after her escape to see him and bring him North. She found him married to another.

Harriet fled in 1849. She had been trying to persuade her brothers to escape to the free states.

Three of them tried but became frightened and returned, bringing Harriet back with them. She remained over Sunday. On Monday night a Negro from another part of the plantation came to tell her that she and her brother would be helped to escape that night. Harriet decided that she would try alone for she thought, "There's two things I've got a right to, and these are death or liberty. One or the other I mean to have. No one shall take me back alive. I shall fight for my liberty, and when the time has come for me to go, the Lord will let them kill me."

A white woman had promised to help Harriet to escape. So. Harriet went to her and received a paper with two names written on it.

The woman told her how to get to the first house where she would get help. That night, the farmer who lived in this house, loaded a waggon, hid Harriet in it and drove to the outskirts of another town.

Here he directed her to another station. Harriet travelled by night, finding out who were her friends and following the North Star to liberty.

Of the early morning when she came north of the Mason and Dixon line she said, " When I found I had crossed that line, I looked at my hands to see if I was the same person. There was such a glory over everything; the sun came like gold through the trees, and over the fields, and I felt as if I was in Heaven."

Chapter 3. Leading Slaves to Freedom.

She was free, but she was a stranger in a strange land. She thought of her parents, her sisters and brothers and her friends in the South. "I am free," she thought, " and they shall be free. I shall bring them here! " She got work in Philadelphia, a large city in the state of Pennsylvania. She saved her money so as to help her people to freedom.

Harriet could not read or write. She had to get others to write letters for her to her family. The firstwere to her sister. Harriet herself went South to bring this sister and her two children to the North, journeying hundreds of miles in danger. The second time she brought away her brother and two other men. She made nineteen trips risking her life and her freedom each time.

After the Underground Railroad had been working for half a century the people in the South demanded of those in the North that escaped slaves should be returned to their owners. A bill, called the Fugitive Slave Law, was passed. Thousands of Northerners believed it was more just to defy it than to obey it.

Now it became unsafe for escaped slaves to live in the free states and many of them fled to Canada. Here they were safe, for in 1833 Queen Victoria had proclaimed free all the black people on Canadian soil.

It was in 1851, after Harriet had made her fourth journey to the South, bringing with her eleven fugitives, that she went to Canada with the party.

Here she lived for the next six or seven years. It was very cold that first winter in Canada. She kept house for her brother and the ex-slaves. They earned money by chopping wood in the forest. Harriet cooked for them and helped them bear the cold winter.

In the spring she returned to the States where she earned money by being a cook. In the autumn she again went South and brought away nine more slaves.

In five journeys she rescued thirty to forty slaves. Already people were calling her Moses, and talking of her bravery.

Harriet used to guide her parties of fugitives by the songs she sang as she walked along the roads. She knew that no one would notice what was sung by an old black woman. Once she left her party of slaves hidden in the woods while she went to find food. She told them that she would warn them of safety or danger by the song she would sing. As she neared them she sang five verses of " Hail;, Oh Hail, ye happy spirits." They understood that if she sang this twice it was safe for them to come out of their hiding place. If it was not safe she told them this by singing one verse from the spiritual, " Go down, Moses:"

Moses, go down in Egypt,
Tell old Pharoah, let me go;
Hadn't been for Adam's fall.
Shouldn't have to have died at all.

It was at this time of struggle and hope for the Negroes of America that spirituals were bom. They came from the hearts of the slaves.

Once Harriet was guiding a valuable slave named Josiah Bailey. A large reward had been offered for his capture. This did not daunt Harriet, for a large reward for her capture had also been offered. In fact once she was found by her friends asleep in the park under a sign advertising this reward; it meant nothing to her as she couldn't read ! When a friend said to Josiah,

"I'm glad to see the man whose head is worth $1,500" he lost all hope that he would escape.

There is a bridge between the United States and Canada. Halfway across this the United States ends and Canada begins. When they crossed the line and were in Canada, Harriet shouted " Joe, you're free!"

Josiah looked up. He raised his hands, and with tears streaming down his face he sang:

> *Glory to God and Jesus too,*
> *One more soul is safe!*
> *Oh, go and carry the news.*
> *One more soul is safe !*

In 1875 Harriet decided to live in a small town called Auburn in New York state. A little place was provided for her by the Governor of the state. Here she brought her old parents. Word had come to Harriet that her father was in trouble. He was arrested for helping a slave to escape. In order to rescue him Harriet needed money. She said, "I am not going to eat or drink till I get enough money to take me down after the old people." She went to the offices of those trying to end slavery and asked for twenty dollars. They had not enough. Harriet sat down and went to sleep. She slept in the office all morning and all afternoon. Friends raised sixty dollars for her that afternoon and she went to rescue her parents.

This was Harriet's most dangerous journey. Her parents were not able to walk long distances. So she got an old horse and a pair of wheels with a board on the axle to sit on. Thus she got her parents to the railway, put them in the train and herself drove on to the next meeting place. There were so many slaves escaping from this region that slaveholders watched all Negroes. But they could not keep them for in the

South, especially in the state of Maryland, there were many people who were in favour of freeing the slaves.

About this time Harriet received aid for her work not only from friends in the states but from Canada, and from Scotland and Ireland.

She made trips through northern states to meet people who were working to free the slaves. On one of these trips in the state of New England she visited Colonel Higginson, who wrote to his mother: " We have had the greatest heroine of the age here, Harriet Tubman, a black woman, and a fugitive slave, who has been back eight times secretly and brought out in all sixty slaves with her, including all her own family, besides aiding many more in other ways to escape. Her tales of adventure are beyond anything in fiction and her ingenuity and generalship are extraordinary. The slaves call her Moses. She has had a reward of twelve thousand dollars offered for her in Maryland. She has been in the habit of working in hotels all summer and laying up money for this crusade in the winter. She is jet black and cannot read or write, only talk . . .."

It was near the time when the rebellion at Harper's Ferry, to liberate the slaves, took place. John Brown, an elderly white man who led the rebellion, had asked Harriet about the Underground Railroad which he planned to use. When he first saw her he called her General Tubman. To a friend he said, " I bring you one of the best and bravest persons on this continent —General Tubman, as we call her." Harriet gave John Brown what information she had. But this expedition failed.

Harriet was in and near Boston in the spring of 1860. She visited the homes of well-known people working against slavery. She told her friends of her experience as a slave and her escape to freedom. She sang the songs and danced the dances of her people.

The men and women who listened to her and watched her learned that black people had gifts which would make the world richer.

Chapter 4. With the Union Army.

1860 was the year of the election of Abraham Lincoln as President of the United States. After Lincoln was elected Harriet decided to go again to the South. She went in December, 1860. In spite of the great dangers she brought away seven fugitives.

After that her friends would not allow her to take such risks.

In the spring of 1861 war between the states broke out. During the summer and autumn slaves were escaping regularly to the Union Army of the North. Harriet followed this army as it marched through Maryland. She encouraged slaves to escape and cared for them in the camps of the Union Army.

Later so many Negroes came that General Sherman asked the North for people to help the ex-slaves to adjust themselves to new conditions. Immediately Freemen's Aid Societies were formed in the North, and men and women volunteered for service among the black people.

Harriet believed that slavery was at the root of the fight between the North and the South. She said to a friend:

"They may send the flower of their young men down South, to die of the fever in the summer and the ague in the winter. They may send them one year, two years, three years, till they tire of sending or till they use up the young men. All of no use. God is ahead of Mr. Lincoln. God won't let Mr. Lincoln beat the South till he does the right thing. Mr. Lincoln, he is a great man, and I'm a poor Negro; but this Negro can tell Mr. Lincoln how to save the money and the young men. He can do it by setting the Negroes free. Suppose there was an awfully

big snake down there on the floor. He bites you. You send for the doctor to cut the bite; but the snake, he rolls up there, and while the doctor is doing it, he bites you again. The doctor cuts that bite, but while he's doing it the snake springs up and bites you again, and so he keeps doing till you kill him. That's what Mr. Lincoln ought to know."

In May 1862, Harriet went to the South. She travelled on a Government transport to Beaufort, a city in North Carolina, where many ex-slaves were gathering. These Negroes had not heard of Harriet.

All they knew was that she had come from the North. They watched her to see if she were really their friend. She was allowed to draw rations as a soldier. But she saw that the Negroes were becoming jealous, so she gave up this right and supplied her needs by selling food.

The small sum of money she received from the Government during her service of more than three years she spent on building a washhouse. Here she taught the freed women to do washing, so that they might learn to be self-supporting. Most of her time she nursed the sick.

Harriet nursed white as well as black people. At one time she was sent to Florida, where men were "dying off like sheep " from dysentery.

She also nursed many who were ill with smallpox and other contagious diseases although she herself had never had these diseases.

She worked till late at night, then she went home and prepared food which she paid an ex-slave to sell for her to provide her support.

During the winter of 1862-1863 a negro regiment was organized and the troops trained. Then Harriet became a scout and spy for the army.

She chose black people familiar with the region, and soon had under her command nine scouts and river pilots. It was their duty to give information about the number of enemy troops, the number of slaves on plantations, and the defences set up on land and water. This information led to a number of successful expeditions by black soldiers led by Colonel Montgomery under the guidance of Harriet. In one of these eight hundred slaves were brought away without the loss of a man.

There was a large refugee quarter for the many black people who had to be taught, fed, clothed and given work. To her scouting and nurse's duties Harriet added looking after these refugees. Officers in the Union Army showed great respect for her, always touching their caps when meeting her. Harriet had to carry letters to prove who she was.

One of these, written by Colonel Montgomery, says: "I wish to commend to your attention Mrs. Harriet Tubman, a most remarkable woman and invaluable as a scout."

Harriet was worried about her parents and was in need of rest. In May 1864, she went to Auburn where she was taken ill. Many of her white friends came to her home and brought her food. When Harriet was strong enough she was appointed niirse or matronof a hospital for black people. Here she remained until after the war was over.

When Harriet was about fifty years of age she thought she would settle down to care for her parents.

She now had a chance to work in the garden and plant trees. The aged and the poor came to her in their need. She welcomed and fed them, and nursed the sick. Her friends helped her with money, food and clothing. Then she raised money for freed slaves.

One of her friends whom she asked for a subscription said, "Harriet, you have worked for others long enough. It is time you should think of yourself. If you ask for a donation for yourself I will give it to you; but I will not help you to rob yourself for others! " But no poor helpless creature was ever turned from her door, although very often she had no idea where the next meal was to come from. She took an active part in the church to which she belonged and founded a home for aged and poor people.

In the spring of 1869 Harriet remarried. It was said that her husband, Nelson Davis, suffered from tuberculosis and that she married him to take care of him. He was a former slave who had fought in the war. He died eighteen years after their marriage.

Chapter 5. Last Days.

In the years after the war Harriet and her friends had been trying to get the Government to pay for her services as a scout and nurse and later to pension her.

Before this was done, she heard from Queen Victoria, who sent her a *Diamond Jubilee* medal and invited her to come to England. Harriet said, " It was when the Queen had been on the throne sixty years she sent me the medal. It was a silver medal about the size of a dollar. It showed the Queen and her family."

The letter she received with the medal "was worn to a shadow, so many people read it."

Harriet had always dreamed of what a fine community farm the twenty-five acres of land she could see from her house would make. The land was to be sold by auction. Harriet, the only black person present, outbid the others. These acres and her home she gave to her church. Harriet called it the "John Brown Home." From that time on until her death ten or twelve persons were always sheltered there.

Another home for aged and poor black people was founded in Boston where Harriet so often went to visit her white friends who helped her in her work. This home is called the Harriet Tubman Home and is still in existence. There are now other such homes in different parts of the United States.

On Sunday, June 25, 1911, an important New York paper had an article in it about Harriet who had been ill in the home she had founded. It was called "Moses of Her Race Ending Her Life in Home she Founded" and said, " She was the friend of great men, but now she awaits the last call.

With the weight of almost a hundred years on her shoulders, she seeks rest during the few remaining days . . ..”

The last time Harriet went to church she said : “ I am nearing the end of my journey .... I can hear the angels singing, I can see the hosts a-marching, I hear someone say :’ There is one crown left and that is for Old Aunt Harriet and she shall not lose her reward.’ “

She died on March 10, 1913.

A year after Harriet’s death Booker T. Washington and white leaders of Auburn unveiled a bronze tablet to the memory of Harriet.

This was afterwards placed on the front entrance of the County Courthouse.

It is a tribute of the citizens to Harriet’s services to the nation during the Civil War, and to her own people in the cause of freedom.

Photograph of Harriet Tubman, her husband Nelson Davis, and their adopted daughter Gertie. Tubman stands on the left holding a round pan. Image courtesy of Smithsonian National Museum of African American History and Culture.

Harriet Tubman in 1911.
Image courtesy of the Library of Congress.

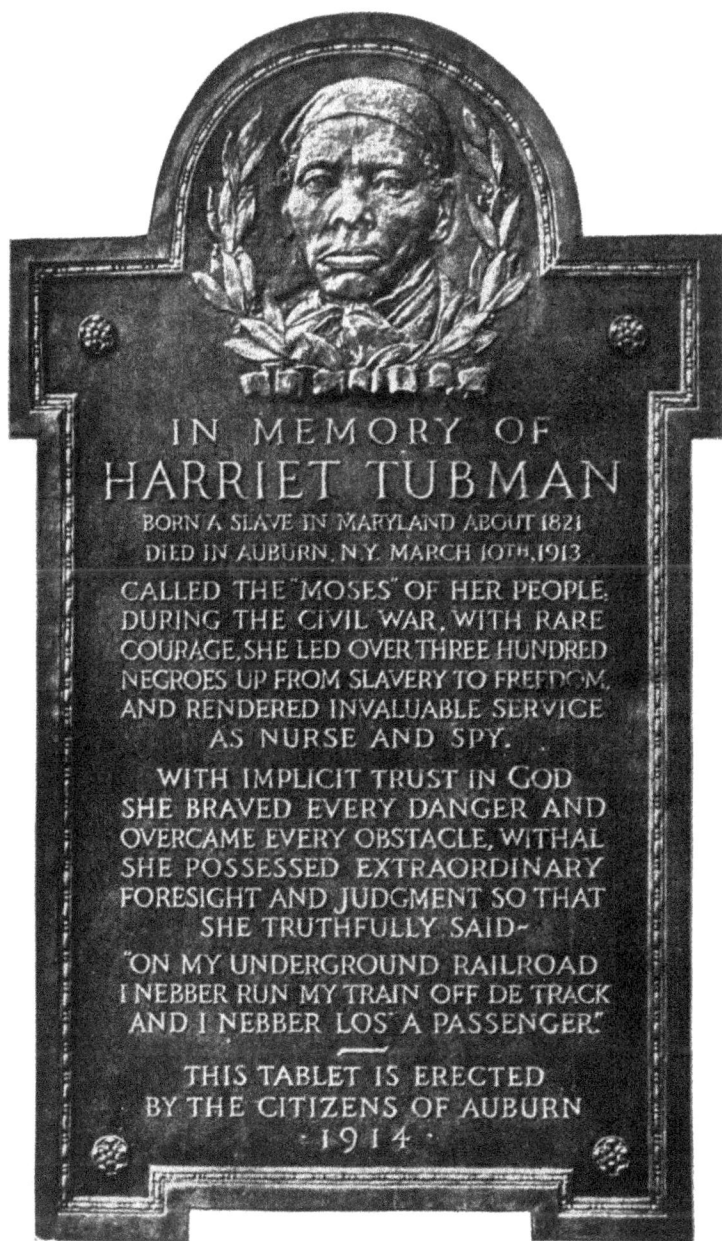

IN MEMORY OF
HARRIET TUBMAN
BORN A SLAVE IN MARYLAND ABOUT 1821
DIED IN AUBURN, N.Y. MARCH 10TH, 1913

CALLED THE "MOSES" OF HER PEOPLE,
DURING THE CIVIL WAR, WITH RARE
COURAGE, SHE LED OVER THREE HUNDRED
NEGROES UP FROM SLAVERY TO FREEDOM,
AND RENDERED INVALUABLE SERVICE
AS NURSE AND SPY.

WITH IMPLICIT TRUST IN GOD
SHE BRAVED EVERY DANGER AND
OVERCAME EVERY OBSTACLE, WITHAL
SHE POSSESSED EXTRAORDINARY
FORESIGHT AND JUDGMENT SO THAT
SHE TRUTHFULLY SAID~
"ON MY UNDERGROUND RAILROAD
I NEBBER RUN MY TRAIN OFF DE TRACK
AND I NEBBER LOS' A PASSENGER."

THIS TABLET IS ERECTED
BY THE CITIZENS OF AUBURN
· 1914 ·

Harriet Tubman tablet.

Image courtesy of the New York Public Library.

www.ingramcontent.com/pod-product-compliance
Lightning Source LLC
Chambersburg PA
CBHW052035030426
42337CB00027B/5020